CW01033563

Aura Of Life

Edited by Heather Killingray

First published in Great Britain in 2006 by:
Anchor Books
Remus House
Coltsfoot Drive
Peterborough
PE2 9JX
Telephone: 01733 898102
Website: www.forwardpress.co.uk

All Rights Reserved

© Copyright Contributors 2006

SB ISBN 1 84418 444 2

Foreword

Anchor Books is a small press, established in 1992, with the aim of promoting readable poetry to as wide an audience as possible.

We hope to establish an outlet for writers of poetry who may have struggled to see their work in print.

The poems presented here have been selected from many entries, and as always editing proved to be a difficult task.

I trust this selection will delight and please the authors and all those who enjoy reading poetry.

Heather Killingray

Editor

Contents

The Poems

Sitting With The Soul

Soaking in the summer sun
Beneath God's leafy trees
Taking in the healing rays
The gentle cooling breeze

Comfort for the body
Restfulness for the soul
Recharging and uplifting
Making one feel whole

To spend an hour just sitting
Amongst the garden flowers
Reminded of the beauty
That every day is ours

We spend so much time pondering
Of the material things in life
Working harder to achieve
Courting stress and strife

I ask you to each day my friend
To gaze at God's blue sky
To feel the earth beneath your feet
For time will pass you by

Take time to paint, to read, to write
And especially to love
Wrap your people in your arms
They are gifts from God above

The water that we drink off
The very air we breathe
Are fundamental to our lives
Yet cost nothing to achieve

God's simple gifts are there to see
If we only take the time
The colours and the beauty
That each day are yours and mine.

Elizabeth Slater Hale

A Sailor's Day

A breeze begins across the sea
Ships afloat so easily
The waves are low, so very slow
Harbour tugs with ships in tow
Frigate carrier mtbs'
Battleships, liner, ferries too
Manned with male and female crew
The breeze is changing to a wind
Getting stronger the sea more choppy
Ship's crew is not quite so happy
Waves now are very high
Ships' bows point towards the sky
Now the stern is going up
Blow hard the wind is now gale force
Coast guards ready for a mayday
Read their maps for a safer course
The weather reports the wind is easing
Waves are lower, things much slower
Clouds are gone, the sun is out
To everyone it's much more pleasing
Get home now, tied up in dock
Another day gone around the clock
Time for a celebration.

Dugald McIntosh Thompson

Follow Me, Follow Me

(Dedicated to my grandson Ryan born 9.4.1991)

Follow me, follow me on the wings of a dove,
Soft whispers blown in on a breeze from above.
Too young and innocent - not touching the Earth,
Too fragile to even contemplate birth.
Imperfections are mortal, so leave them behind,
Tiny souls pure and gentle are the heavenly kind.
Not touched by trauma of life before death,
Just bypassed the world without taking a breath.
Soft delicate skin, with an angelic face
Held close by the Lord in eternal embrace.
Unknowing the life that the family mourn,
Of the hurt and the loss of a baby stillborn.

Audrey Harman

I Remember!

When the flowers bloom
And where rivers flow
And your heart lies in rest

You did not die,
But rest awhile.
Heaven opened wide its arms
To receive your pure and gentle soul
Until once more you awake!
I remember.

What love therefore is greater than mine,
Another simple soul who awaits
The call!
And therein to lie within your arms,
Forever in peace.
I remember.

Bill Clements

Father, Son, Brother, Friend

Father, son, brother, friend,
A man on all, we could depend

Always smiling, a heart of gold
When Martyn was born, they broke the mould

Always helpful, he'd work all day
To his family, he gave his pay

He adored his family, they were his life
Martyn was witty, funny, sharp as a knife

A cloud came over the day he passed
Hurting all the souls here amassed

All have come, to share their sorrow
This bitter pill of death we swallow

We all have lots a little part
Something broken from our heart

The pain we feel, cuts so deep
Sweet fond memories we have to keep

Memories of Martyn's days
He touched our hearts in different ways

Childhood friends, memories safely hidden
Maybe somethings slightly forbidden

He'd smile sometimes, face all aglow
Saying, 'I done that with so and so.'

Nothing hurtful, nothing bad
That's what makes his passing sad

Many loves in his life, he'd say, 'Rock music's cool.'
His love of sport, his beloved Liverpool

Dale's boxing, Cally dancing, his family filled his heart
That's why it hurts, till death do us part

A thought to help you through the pain
Is that you'll all meet up again

And through tearful eyes, sweet laughter will burst
As Martyn's spirit says, 'I beat you, I got here first.'

Carl Fricker

Jimi Hendrix At Monterey 1967

The trick is
to perform primeval ritual sacrifice
with a guitar
and some Ronson lighter fluid on ITV
at teatime

The guitar
both knowing and naïve
in the artist's loving hands
will sing of its own accord
but first it is to be pulled
stringwise
across the body of the trusted amplifier
charging feedback emotion
from another dimension
that is purification

The ceremony of fire begins.

Burned, battered and abused
its back is finally broken
and thrown to an urgent tribe
that gasps with a new elation

His ancestors are calling from afar
inside his own head.

For now, me and him make a pair.

The kids are smoking pipes of peace
There is magic on the air.

Gary Austin

Woodland Symphony

(Dedicated to all at Forward Press on 16 great years!)

What's playing the tune
That the trees dance to?

It is the flute,
In the lilting breeze.
It is the piano
Its keys the rising wind.
It is the violins
In the screaming hurricane.
It is the trumpet
Heralding the storm.
It is the guitar
Strumming the falling rain.
It is the drums
As thunder rolls,
And the cymbals clash.
As the lightning conducts
The orchestra below
We can only watch
And listen; transfixed
And give rapturous applause
Encore! Encore! Encore!

Jan Hedger

Garden Of Light

Next time you're weary or feeling alone
come see the beauty that goodness has grown,
in a garden where flowers grow without cease,
self-seeded by love and bathed in God's peace.

There's pansies for thoughts that are selfless and true,
lilies of peace and forget-me-nots too,
honesty grows there, upright and strong
and love from the roses just floats you along.

Whatever your favourite you'll find it there
as you stroll in the peace and become so aware
that nothing of goodness will come to naught,
not the smallest smile nor humblest thought.

All sow their seed in God's garden of light
and grow in His love to bloom and delight,
so come to the garden, whenever you're low,
come, see the beauty *your* goodness helps grow.

Susan Carr

M1 Motorway

Birmingham is snug
Behind its high-rises
Imitating LA or NYC
And its oceans
Of Suburbia
Where behind
Rectangular
Modern pubs
Woods go spinning
On Crown greens
The Black Country
Has vanished
Into industrial estates
And silent chimneys
Criss-crossed
By rusty rails
An oblivious motorist
Puzzled by his map
Draped over steering wheel
Fails to notice
The shriek and smoke
Of hydraulic brakes
As a juggernaut shudders
Instructions to drivers
Dance in neon
As London slowly
Makes it way homeward
For the weekend.

Paul Wilkins

Marriage

Two lives are joined together
On this a special day
From this day forward
Your lives will entwine
You belong to each other;
'I'm yours, you're mine.'

It's just the start of a perfect time
To share and enjoy whatever lies ahead
A future full of happiness
A dream full of joy
To give and receive
To comfort and rejoice

To compromise and take part
In each other's needs and desires
To hold and console in good times and bad
To live the rest of your time
And be called husband and wife.

Elaine Briscoe-Taylor

Beauty In Britain

'Mid the mellow mansions down England's leafy lanes
And the little country Churches with their vibrant windowpanes
Lies the heart of Britain's beauty for all the world to see
With its rolling fields and meadows stretching down to silver sea.

'Mid the grand old country houses and the village flint-knapped walls
Or in majestic castles with their spacious halls
Is the pulse that's always throbbing in this glorious countryside
Where the green trees flourish and the little foxes hide.

'Mid the hills and valleys where the wild birds sing
Far into the distance you can hear the Church bells ring
In this little 'Isle of Beauty' all is peace and quite with a stillness
                                        in the air
With the wild flowers' perfume wafting in this land so green and fair.

'Mid the little towns and hamlets you can hear the children play
In tiny schools and playgrounds in the warm midday
'Tis the future of our country where pupils go on learning to love
                                        this land of ours
This our beauteous Britain with all its leafy bowers.

'Mid the busy cities where men and women toil
Or in the quiet country where workers till the soil
Lies the heart of Britain's beauty, 'tis our passion and our will
To keep our country lovely and our freedom still.

Mollie D Earl

My Childhood

Whip and top
roller skates
Sunday school
my childhood days.

Skipping rope
hula hoop
make-believe
my childhood roots.

Two-ball skill
three-ball too
snowball fights
my childhood grew.

Marble swaps
picture cards
Grandma's chips
my childhood balm.

Hopscotch chalked
yo-yo craze
no TV
in my childhood days.

Maureen Steele

Silver

Shoot the silver bullet.
Silver dome shining
the light reflecting
on all its surface.

Creep underneath
silver, vital, bright.
Gold; old, comfortable,
respect comes to mind
blended into one; two.
When words spoken
passed with ease and
predictability.

Silver sequence outfit
twirling and bright
celebrating the years
spent; the growing,
loving, hating together
and the moods.

The different expectations,
the etching away at
each other's insecurities.
The hard times and
times for laughter.

Four purposes to
treasure, share and form.
When the together egos
were cast aside to make
room for new life.
To make for a home.

Still together after
twenty-five years: amazing,
astonishing; no just real.
Put a reality on every
year. Mark out the shifts.
Reminisce and thank the Lord
we've survived this long.

Marie McCarthy

Oh So Fit!

I feel so young - so youthful - so fit
I'm getting a lot younger every day
My friend's often gasp at my looks
I really don't know what to say

I do what they tell me I oughta
Like drinking gallons and gallons of water
I go for walks to keep me fit
I don't even have to carry a stick

I never ever drink or smoke
So there's no chance I'll have a stroke
My blood pressure is extremely fine
So the doctor tells me - time after time

I've stopped mountaineering
That's so dangerous they say
Find another hobby
Get your thrills another way

My eyesight too is excellent
I don't wear glasses anymore
Cos I've had my cataracts done
No more bumping into the door

Life now is one long doddle
It thrills me through and through
And to think that next year
I'll be only ninety-two.

Martin Selwood

Summer Celebration

C ome let's away, it's time to play,
E scape from gloom, reach for the moon!
L et's laze in parks and hear the larks,
E at barbecues, forget bad news,
B reathe air, not fumes and smell the blooms,
R ing bells and cheer for water clear!
A ll life is great, but we must make
T he effort to appreciate,
I n days so short, time can't be bought -
O ut comes the sun, are we having fun?
N o, why is that? Too old or fat?
S witch on this year, summer is here!

S A Mottram

Hallowe'en

She stood there pale,
With staring eyes,
Her lips were blue,
With cold.

She did not seem to see
Me there,
Of this night I was told.

Of a girl who seems
To show herself,
But no one knows
Her name.

But she always seems
To appear,
At the time and place,
The same.

She does not talk to
Anyone,
But every year she's
Seen,
On October 31st, the
Night of Hallowe'en.

Sandie Smith

The Lament Of The Lager King

In Castle Carlsberg our king resides,
With a crown of green-gold tin,
Its silver rings point to the stars
And his head remains quite still.

Our four-crossed flag will never fall,
For it's worn upon our hearts
And when we see it flying overhead,
There's no question where we belong.

Rejoice for her our crystal clear
Pure fluted glass crowned queen,
If her drink's at home we never know,
For she's canny that one between.

We buff our tins, we buff our tins,
For the glory of our halls,
For we have no land to call our own,
Since the laureate locked our doors.

We marched to war under pure white cloth
With its golden Stella stars,
But Kronenberg was far from home
And our boats always got lost.

To show his worth, to show his might
He chopped a tin in half
Never to spill a drop, never to swirl o'er top
And all he said was, 'The tin's edge is sharp.'

Our night grows on, our tin shine dulls,
For we approach our sixth hour plight,
His head slumps low, his nectar flows
And our king's tears fill her fluted glass.

Keith Chapman

All I Need

I love you so much
it surely must show
When you are around
You make my heart glow.

Having you near me is more than enough
Our love seems to deepen
Though we've had it quite rough.

I have all I need when I look upon your face
I have all I need should we go from place to place
You are all I want should I look both far and wide
I'll always love you and need you by my side.

Ted Brookes

Songbirds

Songbirds fly and songbirds sing,
Such a sense of joy they bring,
The day is new,
The sky is blue,
Rising sun of morning fair.
Shines the light that shines so bright,
Nature wakes and ends the night,
I greet the dawn
And feel reborn
And happiness is everywhere.

Songbirds sing and songbirds soar,
As mist does drift across the moor,
The ghostly hills,
The eerie chills,
Gently warm as shadows cry.
Colours grey, now colours hue,
Sunlight now is shining through
And so it clears
And dewy tears,
Slowly start to fade and dry.

Songbirds fly and songbirds call,
Within the trees that rise and fall,
Sweet air I breathe,
While colours weave,
Their way inside such harmony.
Willows grow and willows weep,
Beside the pastures that do sleep,
Cool waters flow
And breezes blow,
Across the land so wild and free.

Andrew Blakemore

A Painter's Loving Eye

That the white government
in Washington would heed him
or at least share some of the respect
he felt for the original settlers of America
some of whom became his friends
you would think was the least
they could do
Not even the capital's museums
had wanted
the painter's fabulous collection
to grace their walls
Looking at George Catlin's watercolours
of Native Americans
the way he portrayed them
some in full regalia
others in their daily activities
all with an admiring eye
and a feeling of empathy
you'd wish he had been
the Nelson Mandela of his era
Instead, they erected
Indian reserves to contain
what was left of that great nation
Today you may admire
these wonderful portraits
in lavishly illustrated coffee table books
or go and visit one of those reserves
the way you would go to a zoo
and partake of the shame
of a whole continent
that is, if you still have an ounce
of human dignity left in your bones

Albert Russo

Footprints In The Sand

Who are these people that walk along the beach?
'Which way to go?' is the question they ask.
What are these people thinking?
Hopefully leaving a footprint imprinted on your memory.
But who will reach their soul?

The sea will wash away the footpath that you once used.
Nobody will ever know you walked there.
This route will now be forgotten.
With only your knowledge to compare.
Tomorrow will come, but who will care?

Kate Davies

Goodbye

Goodbye, not forever, I'll see you again
I love you so much my precious friends
I didn't want to lose you
But haven't lost you at all
You're still with me, you're with us all
Maybe not in flesh
But in spirit and thought
You will always be with us

You're such a very special memory to me
A memory as good as one can be
Although I'll miss you for now
I know we'll meet again somehow
But until then
I love you, I miss you
And farewell my friends
But not forever!

Danielle Miller

Mr Frank Palmer (AKA Cary Grant)

Each morning Frank shuffles to the old looking glass
And whispers slowly, perhaps today I might get my wish at last
Last night laying in bed over and over I did chant
Please God let me wake up looking like Cary Grant

He opens one eye gingerly and instead of a bright brown hue
His eyes are still a boring watery blue
Trying vainly to see the whole of his face
He has to balance precariously on a packing case

Then muttering to himself I thought I'd grown a bit in the night
I'm not being too greedy, I only want to be about Cary's height
And where is Cary's hair with its bright ebony gleam?
I've still got my bald spot with the dull dry sheen

And I practised Judy, Judy, till I got a sore throat
And all that came out was Ruby in an unrecognisable croak
He turns and calls out miserably that tanner I left didn't do the job
Tonight I'll leave the wishing fairy at least ten bob

And catching sight of his profile as he strikes a jaunty pose
He seeks not Greek aquiline, but a big Roman nose
But he knows he'll never get his wish
The ladies loved Cary, he sure was a dish.

Frank knows he's going back on a slippery slant
The wishing fairy made only one Cary Grant.

Sharon Beverly-Ruff

Me . . . A Genius Poet

They bin an tell me I have got this thing
I never knew I 'ad, it makes me laugh
seein' wot I am . . . who says it anyway
but people in positions and in't 'alf
as funny as you think, my poem in print
wot makes me famous while I'm bleedin' skint.
. . . and that in't all, they tells me on the side
come read your po'utry: come and 'ave a squint
at geniuses like you who write this stuff
like Shakespeare did, but someone said it in't
that genuine . . . just another racket . . .
you skint while someone makes a bleedin' packet . . .
and in the papers someone bin an' said
it's all a come on . . . only done for cash
and I bin sat with pen in 'and for weeks
keyed up and ready for another bash
but now I've scrapped my souped-up pride and stuck it
with pen and paper in the bleedin' bucket.

. . . but when the trees are silhouettes against an evening sky
and birds have hushed themselves to sleep,
gone home the passers-by
and all is silent 'cept the murmur of a distant train
then must I pick my paper up and start it all again.

Leonard Jeffries

Proud Ray

There was a proud young man named Ray,
Who bought some doors and windows one day.
'But why Ray Bent
When you live in a tent?'
'I own part of a house I can say!'

Joan M Wylde

My Symphony Of Praise

Lord, make my life a symphony
Of praise - an offering.
Remove each strident, squeaky chord
And sweeten every string.

Please keep the instruments I play
Attuned in harmony,
So no discordant notes can spoil
The finished melody.

And keep me centred on the One
Who leads with matchless grace;
And after life's crescendos fade,
Provides a resting place.

Betty Jo Mings

My Daughter, My Friend

(For Dawn)

All the heartaches and pain of the past can't be changed
Nor the untold stories of the future rearranged
But here and now when you need me to care
I will listen, I will help you and I will always be there.
If you start to stumble I can try breaking your fall.
I can hold out my hand if that will help you walk tall.
Your heart may still break, you will hurt and you'll cry
But we'll pick up the pieces together. I'll try
To support and encourage you and help when I'm asked.
I'll not judge your decisions. I'll respect every task.
I can't make the boundaries that are determined for you
But I can give you the space, room to grow, room to view
Your successes and triumphs. Your joys will be mine.
I can share in your laughter; we can sip the same wine.
If our friendship should falter and you choose a new track,
I can only wait for you, pray for you, 'til you walk back.

Only *you* know just who you are in the end.
I just know you're my *daughter*, I'm your *mother,* your *friend.*

Lesley Elaine Greenwood

The Octagonal Chapter House

I strolled past Kings College
In the Strand, on my way
To the National Gallery, to view,
Knights Templars interest
In Leonardo Da Vinci's
'The Virgin of the Rocks'
Then threading the London streets,
In prayer, to Westminster Cathedral:
At the tomb of Sir Isaac Newton,
The Octagonal Chapter House
To kneel, reflect and pray,
After passing Kings College.

Edmund Saint George Mooney

My Love Is . . .

My love is not harsh or brash
Like an out-of-tune orchestra,
But soft like the sensuous caress
Of a wave on a sandy beach.

My love is not noisy or loud
Like the empty sound of a dinner gong
But silent like the secret meeting
Of eyes that says it all.

My love is not flamboyant or for show
Like the ritzy, glitzy cabaret act
But gentle like the whispered kiss
That colours each day.

My love does not crave the spotlight
For fear of being forgotten in the darkness
But is constant like the candle which
Burns throughout the night.

My love does not ebb and flow
Like the changeable tides of life,
But stays forever on one golden road
Which leads directly to your heart.

Sue Gerrard

Gone

Summer has gone,
It eloped with the spring
Autumn and Winter descend
Like a queen and a king
And their son, Jack Frost
With his friends Storm and Wind
Cause chaos once more
It is their special thing.
Snow has not decided yet if she will come,
However, if she does, it will be freak and fun.
It is time for parties,
Masks, fire and celebrations,
A witch's delight
Casting spells and revelations.
A new year lies ahead
A time for new resolutions
To tell the truth of the spirits domain
That we all live on
And will come back again.

Donna Salisbury

The Sweet Taste Of Happiness

(Dedication to Anna)

The blazing sun, knocked on my door.
A host of angels, and so much more.
A flight of doves, in pure white.
A star, shining bright, as in the night.
You have that air, of peace, about you.
Without you, in my world, what would I do?
Darling daughter, you are, all of this, and more.
And I am so glad, that you, knocked on my door.
In the stillness, of the morning, I had felt tears of sadness.
But your, surprise visit, just gave me tears, of gladness.
My arms, reached out, and I held you, oh so tight.
I felt, so happy, and my whole person, you did excite.
We sat down, to chat, and have some tea.
There's no place, on this earth I, would rather be.
We hadn't met, for oh so long!
But on this earth, our love, is, so strong.
I know, if I would need, you badly.
You, would come, to me, so gladly.
You are, so beautiful, in every, way.
You're, that fresh breeze, to my every, day.
Do you know, how special, you are, to me?
It's like having, the sand, without the sea.
You make my life, in this world, worth living.
You're gentle, compassionate, loving and giving.
I enjoyed, our wonderful, meeting, today.
But now, you have to leave, and go away.
I long, for the next time, that we meet.
When I, will walk, with air, beneath my feet.
Just hold me close, and give me, a tender kiss.
Until we meet again, *you,* I will miss.

Linda Jennings

Too Late We Stop And Cry

They told us forty years ago, there'd be a silent spring
No longer hear the song of thrush or bright-eyed blackbird sing.
They said the seas were over-fished, that cod was very rare,
Sea-bottom hoovered of all life, we didn't seem to care.
They told us pesticides were used on all fruits that we eat,
That cows and chickens, pigs and sheep were deadly bits of meat
And over the Antarctic, layer of ozone, there's a hole
The Earth is getting warmer from burning oil and coal.
The ice-caps melting rapidly, the oceans rising fast,
Some islands will just disappear, our coastline will not last.
Should water rise by sixteen feet, it's goodbye London town,
But we still turn a deaf ear and care not if we drown.
The world's seas are more acid now from all our carbon waste,
Where shellfish, plankton cannot live, mankind is much disgraced.
The airlines pour pollution on the skies above the Earth,
With Gulf Stream gone and Ice Age back, no life of any worth.
Our planet's getting dimmer, sunlight cannot get through,
Pollution in cloud droplets brings dark to me and you.
Already it's too late to act, too late to put things right,
Why did we trust false scientists and politicians' might?
What made us close our ears to truth? Why were we all so blind?
Destroying precious planet and peace we could not find?
Why were we driven by our greed? Who let creation die?
Oh God, forgive our selfishness, too late to stop and cry.

Mary Lefebvre

The Fast Bowler's Fantasy

I am the fastest bowler in the world
I bowl at a hundred and fifty-three miles an hour
The ball is just a reddish blur
The batsman doesn't see it
The wicket-keeper jumps out of the way
It crashes through the sight screen
The groundsman's in a terrible temper
Cos I'm the fastest in the world.

I am the fastest bowler in the world
I bowl at a hundred and fifty-three miles an hour
The ball is just a reddish blur
I've broken bats, I've broken stumps
I've torn lumps out of pads and gloves
Now everybody's suing me
But still I'm happy as can be
Cos I'm the fastest in the world.

I am the fastest, I really am the fastest
I am the fastest in the world
Nobody is quite like me
I'm the fastest that you'll every see
I am the fastest bowler in the world.

Robert Latham

Sweet Harvest

Stained fingers, varnish wrecked, scratched from brambles,
I release suction, lift the dusty lid and my face gets slapped
sober by cold air escaping.
Frozen fruits of kitchen industry dwell here;
misshapen bags, soups, etc,
and the shed smell soft earth and ripe fruit,
apples in trays, summer trapped in time and ice:
harvest packed and stored. I re-sort Bramleys in old boxes,
take what I need for now . . . sense your worry.

This place does not contain or define me;
rustic bliss has not fixed or tamed me -
I remain this same jumble of misdemeanours and good intentions.
Sure, years, land and echoes weigh heavier here;
but, under this tawny sky, give me October love
in the damp grass before I'll let us drift asleep.

Simone Mansell Broome

Renaissance

Let new voices now speak out,
Exploitation, greed to flout,
Let us share and live in peace,
Goodwill can make conflicts cease,
Let's defend all human rights,
A new day to end all fights,
Live to love, make God supreme,
This is truth, no idle dream,
There's enough for all to share,
Brothers, sisters, everywhere,
Plant a tree and break the gun,
Joy and justice for each one,
Let's join hands and make it come,
A good life for all, not some,
Set me free, let none be slaves,
No more widows on war graves.

One the Creator, one the Earth,
Give the planet a new birth,
Let us strive with steadfast will,
We're on Earth to love, not kill,
Let's have freedom, end the lies,
Show compassion and be wise,
Hear the needy, hark their cries,
Make of Earth a paradise.

Emmanuel Petrakis

In Sight

Driving at night.
Along a winding lonely road -
Driving in the dark
In silence
And lost in thought.
Near to a left-hand bend,
My headlights pointed straight on.

As if . . . not willing for that moment only,
Not willing to just follow the road.
My headlights pointed straight on
Uncovering
The owl hovering close to the ground
Under the cover of darkness.
Its body so still.

Its stretched wings perfectly controlled.
Its mind . . . after its prey.
Unperturbed
By the sudden light.
The grey silhouette appeared, disappeared -
The moment was brief.
The owl is in me.

Just as my eyes saw it.
And it looks . . . like something . . .
From an inner dream.
In me it is hovering
Still hovering
Held back in time
Held back.

Claire-Lyse Sylvester

Silver Memories

Once unlocked, surfing the silver memory box
sends shivers of tumultuous tidal waves that keep on flowing.
Forty-two years. Our wedding anniversary.

A bouquet of red rose proclaiming undying love
held in my shaking hand as I waited to glide down the aisle
towards you, my safe harbour.

My father proffered medicinal miniature brandy, raising
the inviting scent to sip, gulping down the entire contents!
My mother, beautiful in cream with picture hat of woven straw.
Her high heels adding to her height, mock-croc brown handbag
swaying in waves upon her arm. While carnation buttonholes
sighing in the breeze on ubiquitous grey suits.
My dog, his white bow matching his Collie ruff, his white paws
and the white tip of his waving tail, pounding the sound of
                                        undying love.

For such a low profile 'do' church bells precociously proclaimed
                                        our union.
We stood among the tombstones for the picture shoot.
I guess they get used to the sound of surfing upon green grasses
                                        littered with daisies.
The picture survived, it is still here, looking down over me.
Your family and mine. I wonder if you remember.

While I, silver-haired, sit here alone,
staring at a silver screen surfing the net.
Trying to escape the torrent of tears.

Anita Richards

Reflections

Shimmering shapes glistening silently in still water
Colours gloriously accentuated by its sunlit surface.
Reflections of boats, large and small drifting aimlessly.
The masts moving like wavy coiled wires in the watery ripples.
Sun-kissed yacht hulls, dazzling white, streaking like wavering
brushstrokes
The azure-blue sky dotted with white, fluffy, cotton wool clouds.
Such a vision by water mirrors of cleverly duplicated summer brilliance.
Images beautifully painted upon liquid canvas -
Suddenly broken by ever increasing circular ripples
Distorting nature's heavenly picture like a shattered dream.

Helen Sarfas

Time Pieces

Old photographs
Laid out for laughs
To bring my mind back home
Parties always last
Like lost lovers of the past
In 4 x 5 windowpanes.

Old love letters
Cling to me like sweaters
When I kiss the moon goodnight
My heart's too fast
Now in a plaster cast
In a 8 x 10 box of memories.

Marc E Wright

Coming Of Age

Glad the ink still flows,
Like champagne or like wine,
Letters forming,
Words, sentences,
Then the tapping starts,
With the keyboard dancing,
Beating out ideas,
Sharing the thoughts,
As writers' work,
Hastening to greet,
The anniversary,
Of the Forward Press.
With the words spilling,
Onto the page,
Like players on the field,
Each important to
The end result.

Kathleen M Scatchard

Solo

The cost included uncertainty in body and brain
that the lungs would not hold enough breath
the diaphragm would explode or implode, the
voice would clam up like an organ stop stopped
that the result would be a nightmare not a joy
and I would wish I had not offered, kept the myth.

The prize was the moment of glory, the pleasure
gained from audience fellow choir members me
as the voice bursts out in simple crystal clear truth
siphoned from paradise. Not perfect but fears
did not materialise; hopes did. Creation happened.

Robert D Shooter

American Dream

At last my plane has landed
I've come from far away
With trembling heart and empty hands
And I've got feet of clay.

I've come to see America
And all that it may bring
I've just arrived at Baltimore
And heard the oriole sing.

At evening in the setting sun
I've seen the Potomac
When another day has come
Nothing shall be taken back.

All arised at morning calls
It shall be a free land
A sleeping when darkness falls
None shall have a febrile hand.

It's done welcome American
To take my heart way
I'll think of thee America
Whilst I'm far away.

The big chiefs of America
They will still hold sway
The big guns of America
Sound at the break of day.

In the meantime
And all the in-between times
I will hope and pray

In the meantime
And all the in-between times
I will come home to stay.

B McGarry

Essence Of Innocence

Fuel their fears
Take a tip from tragedy
Let them slip into rhythm; let them keep their energy
Taking a stand against malevolence
Against tides of hymeneal taboos lost to silence

You'll know what it is to become an orphan
Independent from a society
To truly know what it is to be alone
When you're living against conformity

Staying strong
Choose to go against the grain
Or climb out of your skin into conformity's refrain
Show how you're a clever escape artist
You've done it once and then climbed back into your skin again

You'll know the innocence that belongs to one
Self-reliant but secretly lonely
But understand that this is how things are done
Unless the world has an epiphany

I've spent many years in the struggle
Fighting against the power of two
Wish I knew if I was wasting time
Trying to find innocence in you.

Steve Morris

New Millennium

N ow is the time we shout abroad,
E mmanuel, Messiah, Master, Lord,
W e need to make His name be known

M ay our strength come from God alone
I ndeed, we need to seek His face
L et us all receive His grace
L ord, we need You more each day
E very man and beast to this we pray.
N ever let our hearts go cold
N urture us as we grow old.
I f only we could be like Him
U nderstand when life seems dim.
M illennium we must all now know
    Our dear Lord who saved us, 2,000 years ago.

Teresa Street

Twilight

In the twilight of my years
I reflect on the past
When I could move much quicker
People marvelled I could move so fast.

I'd dig the garden like fury
And play cricket and all
Now I get shoulder ache
When I throw my grandson the ball.

My eyesight is poor
Need a magnifier for print
Use the word pardon frequently
And my pension leaves me skint.

But basically I'm happy
Doing the best I can
Enjoying the twilight years
Still breathing, I'm a lucky man.

Jenny Bosworth

Seasons

The mist rises like spirits
Coiling and uncoiling
Across the fields
Giving a feeling of isolation.

Birdsong is silenced
All is quiet
And quite eerie
As people's footsteps echo.

The trees are bare
Their branches standing
Gaunt against the sky
Like unwieldy skeletons.

Fields wet and forlorn
In the winter light
As the cold winds
Blow across them.

Autumn is quite
A melancholy time
But yet a feeling of rest
For all wildlife.

But nature has many facets
The wildness and force
Of the elements in winter
Then the gentler spring and summer.

But as it is in life
Without adversity
We couldn't appreciate
The good times and happiness!

Joan May Wills

The Final Tribute

(For Memorial Day)

The sleeping princes of this world are mourned today.
We say goodnight to them over again
with our wreaths and our prayers.
No one knows as well as the family
of one of these soldiers the meaning of Memorial Day.
We see the crosses, row on row,
exclaim over the poppies, but the boy gone from our lives
makes us realise the meaning of it all.
Today we stand at the grave of a soldier again
and in our hearts comes a strange feeling. Wordless.
Is there a wreath large enough to match the beauty
of his devotion to his country? Only one.
It is in the faces of the children carrying the flag.
he loved his country enough to die for it.
He wants no wreath except this -
the flag he chose as his eternal flower -
Freedom blooming forever!

Marion Schoeberlein

The Spiders' Special Party

There were patés and dips
made from beetles and thrips
while wasps had been puréed and made into whips,
and the pastries and pies,
made from crickets and flies,
had crisp toasty termites piled up round the sides.

There were hot soups and broths
made up mainly from moths
and flea fermentations with froth on the top,
served with coffees and teas
brewed from freshly ground bees,
with a sprinkling of pollen from off the bees' knees.

And set out for sweet
there was treat after treat,
like stiffly whipped ants' eggs - they're quite hard to beat,
then squashed bugs in cakes
topped with caddisfly flakes
and grasshopper gateaux and cockroach milkshakes.

There were firefly flans
and snails out of cans,
flown over, express, from the seaside in France,
while the sorbets and ice
made from aphids and lice
were ten pence at Netto - but equally nice.

The brandy kept flowing
till faces were glowing
and the clock on the wall chimed the time to be going;
then they wobbled away on tottering feet,
full of memories, good spirits and food by the heap.

Eileen Caiger Gray

You Are Never Forgot

You re never forgot
It maybe a tune
A remark or a place
That brings back the memory
Of your happy face, the sound of your voice
The foot on the stairs
Oh how we long to see you here
Tears fall when we expect them not
For we love you always
You are never forgot.

Mavis Catlow

Night

Cool on the cheek are the first airs of evening,
Fingers of darkness creep over the lawn
Feeling their way as the dusk ever deepening,
Senses the truth of the daylight withdrawn.
Piercing the silence, the notes of the blackbirds
Bathe the whole garden in mystic delight;
Twilight, ephemeral, slowly slides backwards
Leaving the world in the arms of the night.
Nectar, its magical perfume distilling,
Soothes and excites every nerve in the nose:
Now the nocturne of the nightingale, thrilling
Remnants of day as it draws to its close.
Rising, the moon shafts her fingers of light,
Stealthily stealing the dark from the night.

Vaughan Stone

1979 - The Years Of Me And You

In the thirty odd years since my life began,
I think of the things that have happened to Man,
Born at the end of the Second World War,
The world was so rich but so terribly poor,
Most food was on ration, meat, butter and sweets,
Small birthday parties, few presents, few treats,
The self-service shops have become all the rage,
Assassins kill presidents and bring a new age,
Computers have taken a lot of men's work,
Sad boys and girls with hypodermic they jerk,
Pill pushers, drug addicts go fly on cloud nine,
Love, life and happiness with drugs don't combine,
Don Campbell and Bluebird life came to a close,
The Concorde plane with its long pointed nose,
Plane crashes, hi-jacks, the world is on call,
The parcel and letter bombs made for us all,
Thalidomide children with disfigured limbs,
The same old church service, the same old church hymns,
The atomic bomb with its big mushroom,
Those astronauts that first stepped on the moon,
The decimal money, to learn it we try,
The Arabs their petrol, the price went sky-high,
The old marriage lines, love honour and obey,
Have been changed to run with the world of today,
Now depression again and rationing too,
Where are we heading? Haven't a clue, have you?
Things getting better, I hope that it lasts,
I hope that all bad things are of the past,
Parents, teachers, parliament, who is to blame?
Some kids are bad, but they aren't all the same.

Nicolette Thomas

Dancing Into The Cream Of The Night

You said take me dancing
in the cream of the night

like we did that time
when the music was Jasper Spanish

The seated flamenco women clapped

out the velocity of chattering rhythms

pushing the black and scarlet music
to the edge of our half-conscious world,

exciting the bloody pump with the drum
of temptation that agitated our lustiness.

The partnership of limbs tangled
loquacious, heady, demanding.

We took to the slippery dance floor
where I held the spine of your wet skin

in the stretch of my flexed palm -
you said your heart needed to dance with me

until the silver slit cracked into the shock
of the smoky grey marbled morning.

In charged anarchy, we succumbed
to fog drunkenly and lost ourselves till then.

Vincent Berquez

I Drink A Toast

My life has been changed from once being thought of morose
Or even cold and unfriendly at times
As I found it so hard to express my innermost thoughts
Until I discovered how to put those thoughts into rhymes

But now a whole new world has opened to me
As verse after verse of my thoughts I jot down
About all things that concern me, from wildlife to war
Or famine and the homeless who sleep on the ground

Yet also the good things I have seen in my life
The love I have been given by those who would care
I have tried so hard to impart my own brand of love
To anyone I have known who was willing to share

The silent tears I have cried over sad things I've seen
As my journey through this life I have wandered
All now written down to share with the world
So no memory good or bad has been squandered

So, on this anniversary of the new poet's friend
I'll toast those who have freed my mind from stress
And any person who like me who wish to show gratitude
Raise your glass to those who work at Forward Press.

Don Woods

Returned To Me

Now -
You take me in
Now -
My love returns

Now -
You breathe my love herein
And only
Now -
Forever will it burn.

April Dickinson-Owen

The Second Coming

Jesus comes again, in His glory, reigning
Not as infant born in a lowly manger
But with angels heralding His arrival
All eyes now see Him!

Those who love Him, greet Him with adoration;
Those who scorned Him, trembling and deeply wailing
Now believe He truly is God incarnate -
Falling in worship.

This will be a glorious day from Heaven:
Saints and martyrs, all who have gone before-hand
Seeing Jesus, crucified once, but now in
Majesty wondrous.

Edith Bright-Butler

Solitude

I'm not alone while walking
Through the heather on the hill,
In solitude perhaps
When all around is still.
But never by myself,
Where nature so abounds
To spread before my eyes
The beauty so profound.

I am not alone while listening
To the buzzing of the bees,
I may be by myself,
But the more I look I see.
The perfection of the insects,
As they settle on the flowers,
I am happy just to listen
In my solitude for hours.

I'm not alone while sitting
On the wild and blowing banks
And I join the birds in praising,
As they sing and give their thanks.
For the beauty that surrounds us,
The companions that we meet,
To some I may be lonely
But my solitude is sweet.

Vanda Gilbert

Fifty Years

You've been married for fifty years,
Together through the hard times and the tears.

You've been married for fifty years,
Together you've faced all your challenging fears.

You've had your ups and your downs,
You've had your smiles and your frowns.

So just think back to the day you got married,
A long white dress and a golden carriage.

But that was in the olden times,
Fifty years have passed since those church bells chimed!

Katie Fensome (10)

Tears In The Shadow

The shadow is miserable on the wall
It reaches out for the door in the hall
But the door is locked and has no key
Gone are his hopes of being free.
Shadow notices the windows have bars
Not the sort which glisten under night-time stars
But like those fixed into the brain
Your energy has gone and can never come back.
Too many years have been spent on trouble's track
The heart no longer has a hunger to live
Love is dead, it can find no more to give
Dreams have vanished under a cloud of grey
For your grief nobody has had to pay
From the sadness you hope to break free
But in the door - there is no key
So shadow takes his owner to bed for some sleep
Lies quietly and listens to him weep.

Graeme Doherty

Hope

Hope keeps us trying,
When we're ready to stop.
Hope keeps us going,
When we're ready to drop.
Hope is that feeling,
From deep down inside
That gives us the courage,
For things not yet tried.
Hope motivates us,
It conquers our fears.
Hope always stays with us,
Down through the years.
Hope is our bible,
Hope is our soul.
Hope keeps us working,
Towards our ultimate goal.
Hope separates us
From most forms of life.
Hope keeps us going
Through all pain and strife.
Hope is our wishes,
Hope is our dreams.
We all keep on hoping,
Or so it seems.
Hope fills our desires,
It keeps away dread.
The day we stop hoping,
We're better off dead.

Jay Berkowitz

Time Tickers

Where has this year gone to?
The months rolled round and round,
Four seasons turned full circle,
End with snow upon the ground.
It doesn't seem five minutes,
Since we toasted in the year,
With glass of wine
And auld lang syne,
And lots of festive cheer!

The calendar turns over,
As each month passes by,
To awaken my attention,
To those dates to catch my eye.
You know, those special birthdays
And plans that you've mapped in,
For days that are so busy,
You might need a glass of gin!

The weeks roll round
And turn to months,
That form to make the year,
Then suddenly it all has gone,
The year has disappeared.
I blame the man who made the clocks,
For he invented time,
It's taken the fun right out of life,
So I've stopped winding mine!

M Wilcox

Siren (1998)

Looking out my window,
I saw, walking down the street,
A siren.
I saw a hundred other men
Looking too.
Long legs and low heeled, walking,
She floated like a song
And was gone.
She was a Sixties figure, a sha-la-la girl . . .

Now she's almost past it:
Her home: a boarding house,
Where the old men fall head over heels over her,
The young bachelors get in her way
And children are never seen.

Every morning at seven-forty
She dolls herself up good and proper
Like the Shrimp, or Twiggy -
Goes to work, on an egg,
Then at evening laughs with her beau,
Another improbable Sixties figure, who has a job
Running a transport and bikers café,
Two bacon rolls, two teas, cheers.

John Goulding

Moment

As I sit here and ponder my thoughts
The fire spits and pops,
Glowing orange and white,
The wood of yesterday's doors
Pine from the floors
A sobering hue radiating heat,
I sip my tea thinking of thee
Sat near here drinking lager or beer
On a beach by a fire for that I now desire.

A sizzle and pop the paint on the wood
Like fat heating in a pan cooking on open fire,
Such things I ponder deep in wonder
A picture of a possible past
A quandary shall I ask it of you
Sweaty skin stuck to my clothes
The fire grows roasting hot.

My tea all but gone;
I take an ember to light my roll-up
And slowly ponder over you
The woodpile shrinks as more thoughts me thinks
Maybe I shall ask you on a date and wait.

K M Clemo

Smelly Memories

In Stokes' coffee house I dwell
When I smell that coffee smell
The smell of coffee wafting all around
As we shopped around the town.

When I smell bacon on the breeze
I'm wafted back with greatest ease
To the grocer's years ago
The bacon slicer on the go.

The smell of butter takes me back
To watch patterns forming on the pat
See it then expertly wrapped
The ladies all had quite a knack.

When its lavender I smell
I smell the hedge where I did dwell
When smell of tar comes to me
A steamroller is what I see.

When creosote assails my sense
I see Dad putting it on the fence.
When I smell the smell of chalk
Again I hear my teachers talk.

To smell the grass now I know
Takes me to fields I played in long ago.
To smell the smells of memory
Is so very dear to me.

Stroma M Hammond

Old Age

She sits alone in her cage,
Looking at television some days,
She peeps through the curtains now and then,
Watching people with their friends,
She wonders if she'll ever have human contact again
As her books and her cat are her only friends;
People she knew died long ago,
And she feels that life is her foe.

Life battles outside her walls,
But he cannot break in and slay her
As the old soldier's sorrows have made her strong,
At a burglar she brandished a hammer,
She sighs and wonders what's gone wrong
With a society that has decayed,
She feels it's infested with worms,
And is plagued by dangerous germs.

She pulls the curtain across the window,
Puts on the lamp and decides to read,
She hears children outside cry
So switches on the radio to drown out the sound,
She hears drug addicts getting high
So puts on headphones and listens to *Beethoven's Fifth,*
She feels relaxed and calm,
Life can do her little harm.

Sarah Sidibeh

The Path Of Life

I don't know why I've been chosen
But I feel the strength
To do what must be done
I've looked God in the eyes
Felt the surge of energy
I shall be released
The sweet sound of morning
Will wash my soul in peace.

Golden are the shoes I wear
To dance now to His song
In the afterlife I follow
Through the darkness to the light
I shall find great comfort
Love will rescue me
How can I alone be worth
The price of being free.

Dance until I'm found again
In death we shall be saved
Then the world will breathe
A fresh and radiant air
All will be revealed
To those who turned away
The dark will surely end
And I'll rejoice the day.

Through celebration of my life
My death will be a guest
First of all a stranger
Until eventually a friend
That I've no need to fear
For indeed it's meant to be
In the stars it's all been written
And this path was meant for me.

R Moir

Hogmanay

You don't have to prove yourself to me.
Your sang sting chauvinist like a bee,
I saw through your saccharine honey,
On the spark-filled night of Hogmanay!

The firework display went off outside,
Our screams heard: when the screeches did subside,
I could not see the truth petrified,
But when I did: I cried and cried.

The seasonal haggis passed around,
We all listened from grassy mounds,
To the bells all over town,
From *your* finger I fell unwound!

You sliced your thumb on a broken glass,
I glimpsed what was inside at long last!
Beauty was only skin deep; blood grass,
You destined as a slice of my past.

Everybody held rejoice in their song!
As Big Ben belted out his *bing-bong,*
I knew I was right and you were wrong!
Hogmanay: when I escaped your prongs.

Sarah Parry

About Time

Time doesn't tick
By,
That's false,
It's not true,
It's a trick,
An imposition
Devised by humans
With their invention
Of clocks, watches etc.
It is good,
Much better, 'just to be'
Because ticks and tocks,
Watches and clocks,
Only causes us shocks.
Rocks
And trees
Are not aware of time,
And they get by quite fine.
So,
As regards time.
Forget it and shine.
It's an imposition,
Not a recommended position.
Time doesn't tick
By
In fact -
Time does not exist.
With that awesome awareness
We can be bright and light
And oh so blissed.
So forget time
And shine,
Don't be time bound,
Then you will happily hear
Love's lovely liberating sound.

Joe Staunton

My Favourite Poem

My favourite poem is usually
The one I finished last
This time it is different
Dwelling some time in the past
Having written virtually
All my adult life, I find
There are several writing landmarks
First to come to mind
A poem in the school magazine
Extolling the pleasures of walking
Later, I wrote of undying love
Which did not last so long
My first poem accepted by Forward Press
Was a highlight too
Followed by a series of sports verse
Quite lucrative were they
Now so many things I write
Are comments on today
So my dilemma you must see
I cannot single out one poem
They are all a part of me.

B Williams

The Asylum

The tinker of time steals life from the naïve
As we look back to yesteryear with regret
At what might have been
In the shadowlands of anxiety
Each daybreak meets with trepidation
As dawn meets the dusk
In the troubled mind of the asylum walls
Which palpate with hatred of the confused
An old man reminisces
On the tablets of the day
Which relieve mortal despair in the incantations
Of a burgled youth
Which was kept secret by the elders
Of a family of fortune
In the days before the walls came down.

Finnan Boyle

Goodbye

Our little world is getting scattered
Our cherished dreams are being shattered
As we both watch helpless from the side
If we close our eyes . . . what do we hide?
Drifting away . . . away from me
Torn away . . . away from me
I feel your anguish . . . I feel your pain
Without your love . . . why should I remain?
Don't stay back to tell me goodbye
I can't see that look in your eye . . .

Why do I refuse to believe
That there could be an end to this
My mind still wanders in yesterdays
My heart fails to realise
Your silence seems like a prayer
And your smile is like a stifled cry
Just turn away . . . just walk away
You won't see a drop of tear in my eye
One more ounce of pain . . . and I'll die
Don't stay back to tell me goodbye
I can't see that look in your eye
Don't stay back to tell me goodbye . . .

Vivek Sarma

Tiny Feet

I heard the news today
About an event coming your way
I hope you are happy at this news
And you're not feeling too blue

The joy life brings
To you within
From a tiny seed
A heartbeat speeds

Within they grow
Nine months not slow
They take our shape
And put on weight

When they are ready
You be sure to be steady
And they will begin
Wait for the cry that they bring

Their love will grow
For you they know
So build them a home
For the seeds you have sown.

B E Ripley

Embrace The Wind

You're caught in a tangle
Of another love triangle
For the love that's lost and missing
You're always reminiscing

Another romance has died
And there's nothing but the night
Lovers have left their sting
And now it's your final fling
To embrace the wind - embrace the wind

Life has cut your face
But deep in a private place
It is much more severe
Someone you once held so dear

So for all the love you have lost
Is this the final cost
From the shambles life sometimes creates
You smile as you make your escape
To embrace the wind - embrace the wind.

Frank Howarth-Hynes

In My Arms

Each and every time I see you
How my pulse it starts to race
To see the shapes that make your body
Or the beauty of your face
Never stops at all the hurting
For I do not understand
Why it is that I can't hold you
Feel the touch of your sweet hand

With elegance you pass me
As your fragrance leaves a mark
Like the sweetest days of summer
Whilst out strolling in the park
Your presence it unnerves me
As my heart it skips a beat
How I know I may explode
If once our lips could all but meet

Now I watch him touch your cheek
Run his fingers through your hair
How I wish it could be me
But you don't even know I'm there
It so cuts the realisation
I may never know your charms
What I would give for just one second
If I could hold you in my arms.

P M Stone

I Am Not Just Saying This

Happy 16th birthday, 'Forward Press',
since I first started in 1996, I have been very impressed!
To Rebecca Mee, Sarah Marshall, Heather Killingray
Chiara Cervasio and others
a big thank you . . .
for publishing mine and my daughter's poems
of which there are a few!

I am not just saying this, but you are the best!
I did send one new poem to another firm, but it 'failed the test'!
On my bookshelf I have books from 'Anchor' and 'Poetry Now',
where ideas come to me, somehow!
Aim is to 'promote readable poetry to all,
as wide an audience as possible', however big or small!

At 16 you can do most things now,
so staff at Forward Press, please take a big bow!
Also Forward Press, remain at the top where you should stay
and have a great, 16th birthday!

Barry Ryan

Soul Reflections

Behind your eyes the sorrow burns,
In your look the sadness turns,
Your expression to pain and disbelief
How you feel is written on your face;
In your eyes there is neither love, joy or peace.

Your eyes are the mirrors of your soul.
If deep inside the sorrow grows,
Your eyes reflect the pain,
And yes, sometimes I feel the same,
For you are not alone in this hurtful frame.

There are many who feel just like you,
It's knowing what to say, and what to do to take away the pain.
But there is no quick fix and no short answers to life's suffering.

For my own relief I look to Jesus,
Maybe you will find the same.
Pray to Jesus and stay awhile in this peaceful frame
The peace He has to offer will help you in your pain.

Pray from your heart to relieve the pain
For there is no one else who consoles the same as Jesus
For in His breath there is the kiss of life
And in Him you will find everlasting peace.

Robert Waggitt

A Wheelchair For Me!

Wheelchairs are coming from a country far away,
I've found out the time and the place and the day.
But how will I get there as I can't walk?
There's bound to be a queue because of all the talk.
I don't want to miss a great chance like this,
To get around on wheels would be absolute bliss.
My knees and my hands are raw from crawling,
But if I try to stand, I'm afraid of falling.
With shoes on my hands and rags round my knees,
If I start promptly, I'll be in time - please!
I'm feeling very weary but it's not too far now,
The centre's coming nearer and I'll get there somehow.
There's lots of people waiting near the gate,
I really hope there'll be one, don't say I'm too late.
Yes - they still have wheelchairs and there's one for me!
They lift me in it gently so everyone can see.
Now, at last, it's happening - as I slowly turn the wheels,
I'm really moving by myself - I can't explain how it feels.
Then I'm pushing harder and I'm rolling quite a pace,
The wind is blowing through my hair and brushing on my face.
I simply can't stop smiling and my eyes are filled with tears,
I haven't been so happy for very many years.
When I go home I won't be on all fours
And I will shout to all I meet as my spirit soars.
Someone somewhere has paid for these chairs
And I will thank God daily for them in my prayers.
They do not know what they have done by helping with this cause,
Allowing us the chance of life and opening up new doors.

Rita Hardiman

Love's Harbinger

Life had no joy until she took my hand,
for only then my heart began to beat
and only then I knew what fate had planned
and why, wise Bard, you laugh when lovers meet.
She loves me, she loves me not.

Life had no soul until she breathed a sigh
as I, rude swain, ran clumsy to her side
to see Elysium shining in her eye,
to revel in the passion and the pride.
She loves me, she loves me not.

Life had no thrill until we gently kissed,
stood silently alone and made a vow;
did ever such a love as ours exist?
Sweet Hebe, youth divine, come bless us now.
She loves me, she loves me not.

Life had no peace until, serene and free,
along the Anglian lanes we wander far
and whisper soft 'The best is yet to be,'
and gaze in awe beneath the evening star.
She loves me not - she loves me.

Peter Davies

Wayside Ruins

It was by chance one summer's morn,
I discovered some ruins all forlorn.
Well away from the busy roads,
Across the fields, where no one goes.

Neglected, it seemed, for a hundred years
The painful sight brought forth my tears.
Those crumbling stones with creeping growth,
Did little to disguise the truth.

Upon this spot, far back in time,
Stood a mighty castle of perfect line.
With remnants of walls and well-worn steps,
I toured the ruins and explored its depths.

And as I climbed its highest towers,
I found I could have gazed for hours
Upon the loveliest of views
Great, sweeping greens of different hues.

A silver stream was just in sight,
Flowing, shimmering in the light.
A toytown village nestling there
Between the hills, without a care.

The changing fields were far below,
Patchwork-like they seemed to flow.
And as I stood and admired the scene,
My thoughts turned to what might have bee.

A busy castle, with Lords and Knights
Riding out to defend their rights.
With many a battle taking place
And many an assault on its face.

Its walls survived these and more,
Resisting siege and cannon roar,
Until attacked by weather and time,
Subject to nature and every clime,
The once proud castle of days gone by
Was left to ruin, left to die.

Terry Daley

Spirals

In the tangled web of love and hate
The urge has never been so great
To run and hide.
The trembling hand that reaches out
To breaking heart, a silent shout
Is heard inside.
Ruthlessly, the days march on,
No time to ponder moments gone
With smile or dread.
No rest, no end to stream of sound,
No quiet corner to be found
Inside this head.
Decisions, like the fox in chase,
To flee? To die? To stand and face
The baying hound?
Thoughts, like eagles, spread their wings
And for their prey choose helpless things
While circling round.
The urge has never been so great
To dam the flow of time and fate,
To hold the tide:
But still the fear and constant swell
Of pain and tears - a broken shell
No place to hide.

Michele Amos

Happy Wedding Anniversary

Our wedding anniversary
Has been and gone and all this time
We have been hanging on
Together our love has been complete
Never once getting cold feet

So now you know my love for you
Because today it is true
All day today I'm going to kiss and cuddle you.

Debbie Storey

The Kitten Who Lost Her Tail

There once was a kitten who lost her tail
She said, 'Oh dear, oh my,' and began to wail.
'Oh what shall I do? Oh where could it be?
Whatever now will become of me?'
She'd searched in the cupboard and under the bed
She'd checked in the sink and on top of her head.
Her mother purred, 'My darling, what's wrong?
She cried, 'Mama, my tail, I've lost it, it's gone!'
Her mother licked her tears away
Saying, 'Don't you know what happens when you're at play?'
The little kitten hung her head in shame
She'd forgotten tails go up when you play a game.
She grabbed her tail and lay down on the floor
She would never again lose her tail anymore.

Barbara Rodgers

Gardeners' Work Is Never Done . . .

This warm weather makes those garden weeds grow
so come along gardener with your hoe.
Now there is little rest for you my friend
for a gardener's work will never end.

There are peas to sow and the beans to tie
and water seedlings before they die.
Then prune the trees and cut the garden hedge
mow the lawns and then neatly trim each edge.

Stake the chrysanths, tie in the sweet peas
be on guard for nasty bugs and disease.
Your back may be breaking, your hands gnarled tight
but . . . your garden is a wonderful sight.

Valerie Ovais

A Night Like This

I'm sour milk at times like this
I don't like ice cream made of this
It's not the music in my heart that
Makes me feel so sad. I look at the
Moon and I feel bad. I cry at wolves
On a night like this. I howl out loud
For my midnight kiss. I don't water flowers
I don't climb towers to catch your kiss.
I walked the moonlight with golden sticks
I wave my wand and I make up tricks
I remembered all this. And I was young
Before all this when the moon shone on
A night like this.
I'm not as bitter as I seem, my mind
Is washed and I am clean.
The moon won't strike the bells at dawn
I'll still be born and then I'll yawn
The flowers still sprout their wings
I'll be lost without my wings.
I'm bitter and sad on nights like this
But I'll be all right after my midnight kiss!

David Rosser

Favourite

My favourite poem?
Well I just can't think.
Perhaps it's the one about my dog,
Perhaps my memory needs a jog.
It could be the one about my daughter
Or even about my son,
I'm trying to remember
But I don't think I've a favourite one.
I wrote a poem when I lost my grandad
And another when I lost my nan,
I'll have them as my favourite
I'll have two if I can.
I wrote one for my friend
She needed one from the heart,
But as for my favourite poem
I wouldn't know where to start!

S L Teasdale

A Betrayal In Season

I touched the rosebuds so they would bloom
You liked the red petals more than yellow.
In winter I stroked the hearth to give warmth to the room,
Where you whiled away memories to fill the time,
Between rising and laying back down on your stone-hard bed,
So that your back would be straight.
It never crinkled your pyjamas, but I ironed them the same.

And then in springtime I cleared the ashes
And set out the jonquils to lighten the gloom,
So that a smile played on your face.

And once you even laughed at my joke
And for weeks I was happy in the memory of sound.

And then summer came and we pushed to the beach
And paddled our toes and you worried at the weight,
But I showed my muscles and for a while you were silent
And then you smiled in a quiet sort of way.

We ate our fill on salads and wine,
I loved the time spent to put each leaf straight,
A flower encircling the radish like the loved flowers outside.

And then in autumn you tired and every day I made your mix
You didn't want it, but drank to please.
And I ran faster, worked harder,
Each task a bit easier for want of you.

And then in winter, you died anyway.

Zoe Manley

Losing The Plot

Sometimes my head feels like bursting
with ideas that want to get out
I have to put pen to paper
or else I'll go mad and be tempted to shout.
I'm trying to untangle my feelings
and look carefully to see what I've got
I've read all I can about spiritual healing
I don't want to be accused of losing the plot.
My imagination is running away with me
I wonder what I am here for
Some would say, 'She is out of her tree,'
I wish I could learn so much more
I'm desperately seeking an answer
I know it's asking a lot
Life has to have some sort of meaning
or am I losing the plot?

Jean Anderson

Anchor Books - Aura Of Life

A Royal Salutation

(To H M Elizabeth II, 1951-2002 et sequ)

Hearken - echoes come this way
Of the pageant of the Day,
Of procession strangely strayed
From the city to the glade.
Lining lanes, each glowing flower
Joins to celebrate the hour:
Buttercups with hoards untold
Shining Cloth-of-Gold unfold;
Forget-me-nots and Campions
And Stitchworts are companions
In the nation's colours true,
Flags and bunting red, white and blue;
Hedgerows fringed with Queen Anne's Lace
Fit to frame a royal face.
Foxgloves chimes-and-changes ring
Bluebells tinkle ting-a-ling.
Bishop Ferns their croziers raise
In a pastoral hymn of praise.
Lords-and-Ladies proudly wait
Representing pomp and state;
Rose and Woodbine scramble high
All the better to espy.
Even Primrose lingers on
Pale, though, her strength nearly gone.
All unite in rural scene
The celebration of our Queen.

N D Wood

Testing Through Time - A Beginner's Guide

As soon as you are born certain things are brought to light,
You are prodded and poked to make sure everything is right.
Life is an exam you begin to realise
Nothing goes untested even down to the colour of your eyes.
Little changes for the first few years,
As even at this young age, there is talk of careers.
At four years old, school is introduced,
A brand new bag, uniform and books are all produced.
Throughout these times you are constantly assessed,
Monitored and checked to gauge your progress.
Infant school tries to disguise the fact,
But nevertheless you have to sit the SATs

Primary school is a different matter,
Here it differs from the latter.
Teachers make no attempt to hide exams,
It seems so long since the days of the pram!
Suddenly by Year 6, the pressure mounts,
Teachers rushing around saying, 'These results count!'

Just four years previously, you had overcome this hurdle,
But now they seem more important, it makes the blood curdle.
The next test so to speak is the transition to high school,
Often an entry exam has to be passed - how very cruel!
The first two years go at a rate,
Then Year 9 SATs decide your fate.

The results of which mean decisions must be made,
Desired option choices may emerge or fade.
After these come GCSEs, the foremost of their kind,
The start of the first real test of the mind.
From now on in you have to cram,
Preparing yourself for the next exam!

Ruth Morris

Over Beachy Head

The sun was warm
As we left our bed
And packed a flask
With some buttered bread
The view was fine
We were newly wed
What a wonderful dawn
Over Beachy Head

When I reflect
On the things we said
When our past
Was still ahead
The life we planned
On those chalky beds
Covered with corn
Over Beachy Head

Now autumn's come
As green, brown and red
Meet the blue sea
White gulls overhead
Our plans came to little
Despite all that we said
But I love you still
Over Beachy Head.

Stuart Delvin

Personal Nostalgia

We said goodbye at the airport
To part again was very sad
But joyful memories were felt
Between us all, the good times we'd had.

Going out together to visit new places
Greeted by people with interesting tales to tell
At the Civil War Museum, sets of battles and faces
Of war and peacetime plans to dwell.

Walked in the forests of pine and fir
The trees so tall reached up to the sky
Bat boxes in the branches, not a stir
From the squirrels settled in their dray

Seated on a horse at the stables
'Heaven Farm' by name
Trotted around the paddock
The dogs thought it was a game

A doe deer and her fawn
Leapt out across our path
I nearly fell off - my face forlorn
But when recovered my girth I had to laugh

Having met their new friends and family
Being invited out to tea
Enjoyed luncheon at the 'Bistro'
That was a special treat for me to go

Walked through the mall at midnight
I cannot recall
The purchased scenic calendar
Which will hang on the wall

Enjoyed listening to the young musicians
Who played with such delight
The visit to the Pizza Hut
On that hot and sultry night.

Walked the dog in the early morning mist
How on earth can I not resist
Remembering it all with nostalgia, laughter and happiness
My daughter and her family's move to the USA has been a success.

Gloria Ford

Majella

They are coming tomorrow morn to take her away,
Out that front door for the last time
My wee Majella, my darling wife and I will not see her anymore.
All I have left is her picture hanging on the wall
Radiant in all her glory.
The smile to melt one's heart
Oh why did we have to part?

She never complained, right to the end
Angelic in her ways that was my Majella
My wee honeybee, life was Heaven with her around
No words of anger passed through her lips
Just God's love for all to see.

Aye, my wee honeybee, throughout the hard times
And there were many, she with her love lightened the load
Singing only of God's praises whom I know she is with right now.

Oh why, oh why did you have to dear Lord take her away?
Have you not enough angels?
You know she bakes the best soda bread and tattie farls,
Her apple tarts a treat, she knew a way to a man's heart
Did she not promise we would never part?

Alas, this was not to be, gone is my honeybee, my Magella
In God's house she now will be and I am just left with memories.
The look of beauty on her face, lets me see she has God's grace.
So fly with God's angels my darling.

In my heart you will remain and when my time has come,
Together we will be, my wee Majella and me.
Sleep in peace my darling, oh how I dread the morning.
One last kiss before we part, it's breaking my heart
But I know that your love will remain within my soul
For evermore to be, my wee Majella, I love thee.

Norman Andrew Downie

Death Of A Tree

I looked as you lay,
crushed and forlorn
broken and twisted
I felt I should mourn
for the way you had stood
strong and mighty for years
for all you had witnessed
I cried silent tears.
How once had your branches
reached for the sky
loving, caressing, the clouds drifting by.

I looked as you lay
and sensed I could see
into the heart, of this once mighty tree,
the sight of you there
reached into my soul
and had I the power,
would again make you whole.

And as you lie
just where you fell
a sad and empty broken shell
people will pass and all they will see,
are the aged remains
of God's beautiful tree.

Jacqueline Davies

A Perfect Day

It was a perfect day,
An example of the future for the present,
The weather was fine,
Whether or not
It was all sunshine with not a drop,
Beautiful and serene
Like her dress
Contrasting with summer,
Embossed with roses,
Like a grand mosaic,
To compliment the great architecture that had gone before,
Yes, her apparel was as beautiful and inspiring as her beauty,
conveyed
It was her moment in the light,
The centre of attention,
As she was escorted down the aisle,
As it was meant for her
Yes, it was a perfect day,
The best of my life
And when it was over,
I wanted to live it all over again,
Except it'll never be over,
For all eternity,
As I married her
And I'll marry her for the rest of my life.

Anthony Ward

Wishes

Oh my darling, how I miss,
Your friendly smile and loving kiss.
How I long to hold your hand,
Grab and swing you round and round.
Share those moments that we found,
When you were here Earthly bound.

Now that you have gone above,
How can I send you all my love?
Today it is your birthday dear,
How I wish that you were here.
No card or present can I give
Left down here on Earth to live.

So tonight I blow this kiss
With my loving birthday wish.

G W Bailey

Days Outing

We snatched a day here and there
A sort of 'ramble' with our lunches
Green fields, sunshine, summer days
It put you in a beautiful haze

The air raids would still be there
When we returned to London
Counting our friends as they arrived at the office
Going into the basement until the all-clear

Box Hill was one of those days
We tried to use some Sundays for such trips
Saturdays we worked always
Monday typing you felt stiff
On the whole they were happy days

In winter we went to work in the dark
And came home in the dark
We had to make counting the bus stops
A bit of a lark

So to Phyl, Ruby, Maud, Pat etc
A day like this was a joy
And something extra to remember.

Phyllis O'Connell

Of Me

No mountain high nor river deep,
No journey long or dreamy endless sleep,
No bird in flight to far destination,
Nor raiment or ornamental decoration,
No passion endearing with heart ablaze,
No countenance in desperation gaze,
No material thing nor richness know,
No finer beauty seen in snow-white snow,
'Tis how life in its simple magnificence,
May smite the holder in all innocence,
As with purity within my heart sings,
Of such joy and inspiration brings,
There's nothing either seen or heard,
In truth I give my most solemn word,
That causes my heart to melt inside,
Bringing tears of love to ever abide,
I speak of a miracle, a wondrous dawn,
Holding on to me my first newborn.

George Carrick

Jubilee Celebration

Hang out the bunting, be of good cheer
Let the bells ring, it's a Jubilee Year
Welcome everyone in the nation
To come and join this celebration.

Like a river of gold children flow
As they guide the royal car through the show
While Caribbean dancers set the mall ablaze
In costumes as bright as the sun's rays.

We raised our flags for all to see
While we sang, 'God Save the Queen'
There has never been such a vibrant parade
Such a colourful, magical cavalcade.

The Queen and family stand on the balcony to view
The Red Arrows paint the sky red, white and blue
And in the evening came the firework displays
Over the palace a rainbow waterfall cascades.

It was all in honour of our Queen
Who has served us well for 50 years
So raise your glasses if you please
To this magical moment in history.

Rachel McKie

Happiness

The sound of running water, as it tumbles over stone,
The gift to see the flowers sway gently to and fro,
To hear the birds at daybreak, a baby's newborn cry,
To watch the changing seasons and the clouds go rolling by.
To talk with friends or sing a song, walk through these lovely lands,
To paint a picture, write a verse, to work with your own hands.
To sit out in the garden and watch the children play,
Or read a book sat on the grass on a lovely summer's day.

To watch the leaves of autumn, turning now to fiery hues
Or a snowflake landing on your nose and dusting white your shoes.
A snowman built with such delight, children sliding in a line,
Curled up in front of a log fire, the smell of burning pine.
Roasted chestnuts, Christmas time, giving and receiving gifts,
A brand new year of memories, to give dark days a lift.
A newborn lamb skipping round, birthdays and family treats,
Trees in bud, a snowdrop white, crisp paths beneath your feet.

Friends and family gathered round you, to share those special days,
Making plans for summertime, the annual holidays.
Expected births and christenings, new life around you springs,
Happiness is life itself, that gives you soaring wings.
A child's first steps, a new address, a foal trying to stand tall,
Puppies crying for their mum, some kittens curled up small.
Many things bring happiness, as does happiness itself,
Strong in mind and body and the feeling of good health.

Kathleen Townsley

To My Husband

It seems long ago since we were young
But from our experience lots of things have sprung
The days of youth were good to us
We learnt to struggle and to strive
It taught us things about life
But through the years you've been my guide
My lover, my husband and my child
Through illness, through gladness
You were always by my side
And for each day I say a prayer
To thank God He gave you to me
Even though your hair shows grey
I'll always love you all the way
When you're cross I still know you're boss
And I admire you
Though your faults are few
You have humour, sense of play
With each day a new challenge you display
A challenge for me to do my best
For one of us was better than the rest
Who stayed by my side
Through the rough and the mild
The best father a son could have
You gave him more than money could provide
You have him good fatherly advice
So as the years bring their gold
We learnt a story, a story so old
A story of love and friendship dear
And this has helped us through the years
So hold my hand and keep good cheer
So my husband who gave me so many happy years
You've been dead for 10 years now
But each day you were always there I miss you
To pick up the pieces more and more
May God always bless you.

Mabel Houseman

Anchor Books - Aura Of Life

A Family Mother

Mothers are like cotton wool, they surround and keep us warm.
Fathers are like motor engines, once they start they ramble on.
Then there is sister, nosy and concerned
And brother who is always right.
When put together in one room, you will always see them fight.
Grandfather and Grandmother are the wisest of them all
For they have passed down life's long road
And come out smiling, feeling tall.
Uncles and aunts are just like grants,
You only see them but by bit
Once a year if you are lucky, with all their charm and wit
Cousins, well they are someone who you can't forget,
The things they do without regret,
No shame, no fear, not even fret, the things they do just for a bet.
Put them all in one big pot and outshines mother above, the lot
She cares, she teaches, she feeds and clothes
And is the best thing on Earth as life goes.

Ken Thompson

Untitled

When you find you're facing sadness,
try to sow a seed of gladness
Or . . . take time to share a smile,
why not walk that 'second mile'?
Do a favour for a friend,
try to make your soul unbend
giving always was a pleasure,
to be willing, is a treasure.
Can you give someone 'an ear'?
Understanding will bring cheer,
help another, do your part,
feel the glow deep in your heart.

Lewis Park

Who? What? Where? When? Why?

Who is it that talks with a whisper?
Who is it that shrieks with a holler?
Who is it that walks like the dead?
Who is it that crawls like a baby?

What is it that unlocks the door?
What is it that turns on the lights?
What is it that moves the furniture?
What is it that haunts the house?

Where does it keep its keys?
Where does it sleep at night?
Where does it sit?
Where does it eat?

When does it arrive home?
When does it rest?
When does it sleep?
When does it eat?

Why does it do all this?
Why does it haunt the house?
Why does it try to control everything?
Why does it terrorise us?

No one knows!

Louise Smith

Through The Window

I stand at the window
but I do not see
the rolling moors extend.
A tearful reflection
is staring back at me.

Twisting knots within
pull pain into me.
Obliterate the view.
A woeful countenance
is all that I can see.

This broken pane of glass
now represents me.
Crazed and splintered,
the violence of the act
displayed for all to see.

I stare through the window
but all that I see
is the future we planned,
smashed and obscured,
staring back at me.

Brenda Artingstall

Many Childhoods

I've entered my second or is it my third childhood?
This time round, being young again is really good.
People watch me having a great time by acting mad,
I look at them, wonder why they all look so sad.

Frenetic adolescent worries have disappeared,
A breathtaking, strength-giving confidence appeared.
Not sure I've gained wisdom, older I've become,
Bring on subsequent childhoods, helps beat feeling glum.

S Mullinger

Songs Of Praise

A regular Sunday programme,
That I like to see,
If you hear someone singing loud,
You're right, that person must be me.

I like to join in
And sing the hymns I know,
Regardless of the tempo,
Be it fast or be it slow.

I was in the choir,
My voice they tried to groom,
But I was asked to leave,
As I sang out of tune.

So I watch the programme,
That's called 'Songs of Praise',
Always joining in the singing,
Loudly, my voice raise.

Out loud I always sing,
Although my singing is a mess,
Nobody complains,
My neighbours they are deaf.

People from miles around,
Come to hear me sing,
When they hear my singing,
Their earplugs they put in.

It's a very good thing,
My programme is at teatime,
No one would get much sleep,
If it was on at midnight.

Jeff Northeast

Animals

Fancy being taught and expected to repeat,
animals are here to give us something nice to eat.

The beautiful vegetation was not put there just to view,
you've got to tear and hack it up and throw it in a stew.

It's not enough watching a fish glide gracefully downstream,
dabble your hook inside its mouth and see the blood all teem.

Fluffy, furry creatures jump for joy across a field,
pick up your rifle, aim it straight, from you they have no shield.

But if you want to cause more pain, to fill something with rage,
go out and catch things that are free and put them in a cage.

Those trees are taking up a space you want for your car (new),
though forests help us all to breathe, we saw down quite a few.

Eggs of birds are nice to eat, with them you have enough
casting your eye upon the bird, you strangle it quite rough.

Even the snake likes very low, hides out there in the grass,
until man with his big forked-stick needs handbags for his lass.

Show-off the cows all grazing giving milk to young and old,
push them into the slaughterhouse where death smells in the fold.

Tell children animals are fun and plenty they should keep,
so, cruelty can start quite young, as soon as they can creep.

Jean Paisley

Passion And Belief

In the beginning came an idea
a passion a belief.
In the beginning came a dream
A hope a loan.
From then on you build a foundation
on a support of trust.
Trust if built right is a strong basis
an infrastructure - for the future.
But an idea won't grow
if it's got foundation instability.
What has been brought together
through hard work - sleepless nights
heartache and sacrifice
has now borne fruit
though it will need careful
nurturing - pruning and guidance
it's now strong enough
to weather most tempest storms
injust over two and a half decades
a dream scribbled on the back of
some used envelope - and taken its first steps
as grown and will continue to grow with luck
and with the right scaffolding
good luck for the future - and all it holds
and as Neil Sedaka would say,
Happy birthday sweet sixteen.

L Parnell

To Kerry

I have written you this poem to show you my love,
As far as sisters go you are a cut above.
When times are hard as they sometimes are,
Always remember I'm your brother, I'll never be far.
I will always be there for you till the day I die,
If there's anything I can do for you, I promise I'll try.
Over the years sadly we have been apart,
But never again now we have our fresh start.
From little children we were taught to love and defend,
I promise darling sister to be there for you till the end.
I may not see you for weeks on end,
But always remember on this brother you can depend.
These works I have written from beginning to end,
Are written from my heart from your brother and friend
I love you
Ricky.

Ricky Dabbs

My Boys

J ust to be with them and to stand back and watch them grow
O h how what will unfold on their first steps of this life only time
    itself will tell
H eaven-sent they were, because they are so fine
N o one knows their destiny, but I feel in my heart their path I
    know will be true.

D oing my part to nurture them is a joy and a pleasure
    only a true loving father can feel
A nd already I can take a step back as their wisdom and love
    of people is already there to be seen
V ital they stay strong and keep together, love for one, love for all
I am honoured to bring such beauty into this world
D ays of all days will be a much better places now my boys are here.

T hey will help, love and protect
H ow much I miss them so when I can't be with them
O nly my heart truly knows the whole truth of a father's love
M y mind does worry for them, but I know they are resolute and strong
A nd they will be fine
S o I know this world forever will be a better place because of
    my boys.

Michael Graham

No Hiding Place

Our family are scattered far and wide,
All getting by, making a living,
Doing the best for their part of our clan,
Facing each new day's challenge,
Carrying our family name, with passion and pride.

Like many other families only deaths or marriages bring us all together
Or a chance meeting in Sainsbury's car park,
I'm ashamed to say, I may not speak to my brother for six months,
Then we'll catch up over a pint or the phone,
These conversations have been known to last forever.

Old Granny Smith has not been well, at her age who can tell,
Our Carly fell off her bike onto a rusty spike,
Sharon passed her exams, with top grades, but a job for
                                        her still evades,
Cousin Jim now four stone less he scales, after his mountain
                                walking holiday in deepest Wales,
Dilly our dog died since last we met, for countless years she'd
                                        been our family pet.

Many of ours emigrated around the world, from Australia to Timbuktu,
Our Edwin just had to end up somewhere that crops up in many
                                                conversations,
Most of us wouldn't know where Timbuktu was or if it existed,
But life there is pretty grim, especially for the locals,
Who on a wing and a prayer just scrape through.

In the UK, our family are far flung, from Scotland to Cornwall,
Recently our family tree we tried to research,
But unanswerable questions soon brought us to a dead end,
Fascination but frustrating I found, like our great aunt May,
Who mysteriously died in 1920 close to Luggershall.

Perhaps leaving this mortal coil to treat the world beyond,
Will bring some answers, from your long-lost kith and kin,
Hopefully everything will then fall into place, way back to the year dot,
Questions are answered that have bothered you for years,
As you realise just how vast your family really is,
It occurs to you, that along with everybody else's families
You have a very special bond.

P J Littlefield

In Loving Memory Of Edward Henry Billing

(10/8/1922 - 20/4/2006)

As I walk into the tiny chapel
'Somewhere Over the Rainbow' is playing
I tell myself I will not cry
'Just let go,' my heart is saying

Yellow flowers adorn your coffin
Father John plucks me a yellow rose
I thought my heart would break that moment
Filled with sadness, like no one knows

Holding hands to find some comfort
Tears I hear on either side
Tears that should have been so happy
When I should have been your bride

'All I Have to Do is Dream', is playing
The saddest song I've ever heard
But as I listen to the lyrics
Never were there truer words.

I walk up to your coffin
To say goodbye in my own way
Knowing I have all my memories
And the 'Last Waltz' begins to play

Finally the service is over
It really is our last goodbye
I'll waltz with you one day my darling
In Heaven's garden where yellow roses never die.

Trudy Simpson

Those Were The Days

Those were the days
Always enjoyed by old and young
In so many fascinating ways
Everyone friendly, together having fun

Thy nostrils breathed in pure air from the sea
As folk walked in rhapsody hand in hand
Enjoying a lovely sea breeze
Somewhere heard echoes of a band

Those were the days
Folk seeking friendship and happiness
Every day being pleasant in some way
Folk seeking to do their best

'Twas often the little things
That everyone enjoyed
All that content could bring
Inspiring one with spiritual blessing

Those were the days
Fun and amusement travelling by bus or train
Everyone friendly, happy in array
Enjoyable wonderful days all in the game

Every Bank Holiday during the year
Folk looked forward to a pleasant time
Filled enthusiastically when day was near
The weather always appearing fine

Although time and many years passed
Folk of that era will always
Reminisce wonderful memories that will last
As those were the days.

Josephine Foreman

Injustice

Our world is such a diverse place
With gigantic problems to face
The gap 'twixt the 'haves' and 'have-nots'
Is one of the obvious blots.

Men paid millions to kick a ball
Millions have no income at all
Those lands with huge natural wealth
Pay little heed to people's health.

That wealth is gobbled by so few
The masses wait behind the queue
For whom there is no handout still
They daren't get ill. Who'd pay the bill?

Assuredly they do fall ill
No medicine not e'en a pill
Water's stagnant, no food to eat
Bloated infants with no heartbeat.

Suffering children fail to live
Parents can't help, they've nought to give
Adults, tho' a wee bit stronger
Millions don't live any longer.

Contrast things in lands of plenty,
Where bellies never go empty
Food crops growing with ample sap
In the home, clean water on tap.

There's work to do, wages to earn
Money to spend without concern
One wonders will there ever be
Ways to create equality?

Brian Eley

The Scent Of Violets

The scent of violets filled the air
From whence it came I knew not where
Until I got down to pray
On what turned out to be a special day

I prayed to our Lord above
And the scent came down with a mother's love
As if to say I know you're sad
But I am with you, my bonny lad

I used to sit upon her knee
As each bedtime she read to me
I could smell the scent she wore
Even after she kissed me and closed the door

That same smell was all around
As if the violets were on the ground
My heart felt lighter, my spirits soared
Because of a mother, whom I adored

Her love for me helped me go on
And one day I'll join her in that throng
I'll thank her for the love she had to give
Which gave her son a reason to live.

Diana Daley

The Visit

Fields and cows whiz by
as morning eyes strain
'Blue car, red car,' from the back.
From the front, another blue-white ghost lingers,
then puffs over Dad's head
to ooze out of the waiting window.

Just in time:
her snowy curls gleam;
his sun-soaked face glows;
their clasps bring sweets and welcome.
Tweed, beige, shoe polish, grandparents.
Then hungry rumbles are filled with shortbread.

Soon, the lakeside beckons,
cool and free.
With tweed now cast and trousers rolled,
we plodge
and splash
among shimmering rainbows.
Dark green velvet cushions our feet.

The chequered flag waves; time up.
We sit,
we eat,
we drink,
we laugh,
we snooze.
Then, we do it all again until
our shadows
grow.

Jo Borowski

Nostalgia

Forgotten love songs,
Forgotten names, long ago people
Lone ago games, past is a whisper,
In the shadows of night,
Future is filled with a heavenly light.

Forgotten singers of songs we could sing
Words came so easy as eternal spring
Life filled with meaning, life filled with song,
Life of the young when days were so long
Now remembered forever on the wings of a song
On the wings of a song we'll travel the light
Stardust we'll gather as we wander the night
Moonlight and starlight will show us the way
Chasing rainbows at random till the dawn of the day
On the wings of a song to a melodious strain
We may bring back the wonder of our youth once again
Maybe we'll remember all that was gold
And treasure the moment before we're too old.

A Reed

A New Beginning

Grey slate tiles drip a steady stream,
That splats and patters on the sill,
The path becomes a rill,
The steps cascade away,
We are castaways on this island
And beg our trees to drink their fill.

It rains in Welsh,
'Bore da, bore da',
Its patois patter
Speaks native to the frame,
That screens the silent view
Of the old mill.

The cadence pats and plumps the moss,
Beginning to settle on our stone walls,
That huddle sodden flanks of sheep,
Staring through dripping lashes,
To welcome us
To their hill.

It pats again.

I trace the imprint on the pane inside,
Following each rivulet till,
It pools its pain outside with mine
And washes the slate clean.

Susan Carter

Teens

My teenaged son was such a wreck
oily jeans and dirty neck,
motorbikes and tools, oily rag in hand
with his music blaring, head buried in the sand . . .

Then suddenly there was a change
a girl appeared on the home range.
The music that he used to play
is now replaced by romantic sway . . .

His bike is now placed on one side
for she does not like him to ride
his hair is washed, he takes a bath
can that be him strolling up the path?

A son of mine in suit and tie
she must be quite a girl I sigh,
next thing we know he will be spliced
(must tell her that he keeps pet mice!)

Melody

New Year

As a new year
begins we all excite
at a better future
in sight
out comes the parties
in full bloom
everyone connecting
in full bloom
smiling faces incite
well into the
middle of the
night
till boats sound their
horns
firecrackers incite
excitement
of a better
future in sight.

D McDonald

Nana's Special Birthday

We will celebrate this day,
Thinking everything about you,
We will think about the good times,
To help us from all feeling blue.

We will celebrate your life,
As we would if you were here,
And think of all your memories,
So we can keep you near.

We will celebrate this birthday
And think of your smile,
All your love you gave and received,
Really made it all worthwhile.

We will celebrate today
But without presents or party to go to,
But we always had the best gift
And always that was you.

Louise Chafer

Laura

(Slim cunning hands . . .)

I watch you eating birthday cake
And think of that.

Perched upon a kitchen stool,
Slender fingers elegantly peeling icing from the sponge,
Head tilted back, mouth open to receive the offering,
Sacramental, sensuous.

Your strong young tongue crushes the sweetness, savours the taste,
With all the greedy delicacy of your twelve years.

You are such a contradiction now, not child, not woman,
Wearing youth with exuberant ease.
You move, a coiled spring, with awkward grace,
Innocent knowingness;
Vulnerable, yet secure in the knowledge
That you are the centre of our world.

How did you get to be twelve and I not notice it?
Where is the time I should have cherished, hoarded,
Between this moment and that, when first you were?
What will you be when another dozen years pass over us?
A woman grown; a bird flown?

Christening cake,
Birthday cake,
Wedding cake:
Sweet landmarks for a sweet life;
Nothing between them but a blink from your long-lashed eyes.

Aideen M D'Arcy

Written In Stone

Like blessed Michelangelo
God chips away at me
Hammer and chisel in the master's hands
Marble dust like fallen snow.
What seems the cruellest blows
Are designed to save my soul
David is born from sculpture's gaze
To slay the dragon of reddish hue
And the Father polishes the whitest stone
With tender love, no ruthless eye
Like blessed Michelangelo
God chips away at me.
Oh blessed Earth where love survives
Like a lighted candle in darkest night
I pray come forth white dove of sacred peace
And speak in wondrous thunder and lightning
Let the sweet name of Jesus
Be written on your hearts of stone
All of nature will kneel before His throne
Like blessed Michelangelo
God chips away at you and me.

Thomas Hull

The School Of Night

We study at night
It is quieter then
We turn pages of ancient books
Brushing away cobwebs
Taking care with fragile papers.

We are a band of brothers
Devoted to learning
We profess to speak of high things
Every night we assemble
An eternal flame burns
Knowledge is never extinguished.

We debate, we discourse
Sometimes we disagree
But we continue to push for solutions
To search for a consensus
Then re-engage with the problems
Of philosophical argument.

This school of ours is unique
Many applications to join
Are turned down
We are a secretive organisation
Our libraries are candlelit
We are a serious organisation.

In the school of night
Our thoughts are like torches
We dust down concepts
For re-examination
Taking care with fragile dreams.

Ian Bosker

The Poem

The words line the page
Floating subliminally in my mind
As my finger traces them
My mind consumes them
My spirit absorbs them
I begin to feel them
The words.
Are my new-mined jewels
Are my one ray of sunshine through storm clouds
Are my white roses, I can never get enough
Are the beautiful view I drove past in the country
Are the perfect song at the right moment
Are my first cup of coffee in the morning
Are my satisfaction to my craving

The words.
Are whatever I need them to be.

Rufaro Ruredzo

Part 1
The Truth Will Set You Free

It's better to die for the things you believe
Rather than live for the things that you don't
It's braver to speak out about that which is true
Than keep silent about that which is not.
It's more hopeful to yearn for the things that are good
Than endure the things that are bad.
It is wiser to grin at the prison you've got
Than regret the freedom you've had.

It is nobler to strive for the things out of reach
Than have things to hand by a wall.
It is safer to forget the laughter of friends
When it brings back the enemies' call.

It is more worthy to serve the God you can't see
Than be seated by the gold calf that you can.
It is higher to sit at His feet all your life
Than on a throne, a chair or sedan.

P Cockin

Times Of Rags And Bones

Days of smelly engines, gas lights and trams
Dads were away or had duties to do
Mums worked. When clogs gone. Then the war was won.

Grandpas and grandmas use their skills . . . Time marches on

Boys brum Dinky cars. Girls dream of shiny stars,
Lands on the moon or faraway to Mars . . .
Ours, those building blocks, fine model rail tracks . . .

On cobbled streets folks take home the bacon,
Weigh crispy biscuits, cherries and spices,
Sugar, coffee, rices . . . brown sacks sagging . . .

More bagging sweet treats
More fast planes, slow ships, trains
More recycling packaging

All childhood dreams of themes so long gone by
The hay higher than I . . . in my mind's eye . . .

Bright lights soon flickering . . . queue for a balloon
Times when we see the rag and bone man.

Lesley J Worrall

When Saturday Comes

Through narrow streets and winding lanes
We'd walk through noonday sun
To where working class men, boys and maids
Spent Saturday afternoons for fun

'Read All About It's' on the air
'The latest football news'
We'd scan the sports pages avidly
For Brian Glanville's views

Rosettes and scarves and wooden rattles
Adorn the young and old
Better take a Fisherman's Friend
To ward off flu and colds

Police horses divide the blooming crowd
Toward 'Home, Away Team', signs
As other teams were well supported at every game
Another part of streets assigned

'Get yer programmes here' is yelled
By a booming cockney voice
Whilst tickets for the Irish Sweepstakes
Promise dreams of wealth by choice

'Roast peanuts, roast peanuts,'
In tiny paper bags, are offered to the mingling mass
By a young fellow stood beneath a hoarding
Advertising Olde Holborn roll up fags

Turnstiles clicking quickly
Admit brightly coloured hordes
As 'The End is Nigh' is signified at gates to stadium
By blokes with six-foot boards

Grey sombre streets are brought to life
As floodlights light the sky
Like a microcosm to just that wondrous place
That was dazzling to the eye

We donned our bobble hats and pac-a-macs
Our rattles clacked, as the teams took to the pitch
In those days of so-called abject poverty
Such football memories make us rich!

Kevin Raymond

September In Broughton - 1997

Autumn's chilly fingers touch
a sunny day. The sparrows, nagging
quit this hedge, to carp as much
downhill, where horses' tails are wagging
flies off, to hush those birds' twitter.
Their riderless hours are lagging.

Children, wearing new or thrift shop
uniforms have gone to school -
where now, classroom air won't sop
much chalk-dust up. Computers haul
blackboards into history -
and the awesome mystery
of teachers' handwriting should stop.

Gillian Fisher

Rock Pools

Sea-green pools - in the rocks
Worn smooth with restless waves,
The tide never stills -
Year in, year out,
Can be cruel at times
In winter storms,
When wrecks at sea
Wash up bodies on shore -
Driftwood and seaweed
Toys and tin cans,
Fish nets and bits of old rope.
But the sea can be calm
And glint in the sun
When children paddle and
Play at the water's edge.
The song of the sea is a lullaby
A murmuring sound for sleeping by -
But sailors beware, be on your guard
You never know when a storm is nigh.

Walk on the rocks
Search in the pools,
Where baby crabs and fishy things hide -
Washed with the waves in the restless tide.

Ellen M Lock

Pudding Power

Put them in a pudding,
Stir them up!
Deep, deep bowl
Plop, plop, plop!
Pour more and more,
Cut and chop,
Flip and flop
Stop and mop.
Everything goes in,
All in together,
Churning, turning,
Wet or dry, sweet or sour,
Drop on drop.
The bottom of the bowl
Is a chaotic mess,
I've slaughtered this
And melted that
And shredded who knows what.
And I've enjoyed the butchery
And got them in my pot.
Joy! Power!
I cover and wait
And cool and drool,
Control the contents
Of my bowl.
Now move them to
Another dish
And oven heat them,
Burn them, turn them,
Watch them fuse,
Become as one,
Confuse them,
Use them, then
Gobble them all up!

Joan Blissett

Sunset

The incandescent sky
Deep-throned in cloud glory
Reflects the setting
Of another day;
Lost down time's alley
Now moonglow soft
Virgin clear
On watery willow mirror-pond.

We fish for friends
In mind's relief and imagination,
Stormy ancestors
Of the great God Thoth.
It will form again
From the blackest night,
Shadows, stone circles of magic
Like a Velasquez painting
Wrapped around lover's light
In fields of another hue.
We are near the silk-thread dawn
Of butterflies' gossamer wings
Nestling in-between
The rough-hewn hedge
Of a brown riverbank.

The sound of *plop*
And the ripples ran-out
With midges caught in the act,
Raiders of a silent underwater world:
Wriggling salmon, stationary,
Waiting for another chance
To procure a twilight meal.
Amazon-heads asleep
Under algae tree roots.
Yes, we will find the morning again,
Still, rabbit-flocked and expectant
For another new day to arise.

Peter Corbett

The Good Sowing

Ungrounded in zero,
was it a target
was it a circle
was it a symbol
holding
the eternity
of our conditioning architecture -
a theatre of intimacy
of powerful forces
of principalities and prayers
of flowers tidally flowing
in patterns of silence
knowing the unknowing
world within worlds
never the same again
starts in the mindsets of hearts
- the good sowing.

David Lloyd-Howells

Love Lost

You cherished me once, so what went wrong?
You've neglected me now for far too long
I remember feeling completely adored
But now I believe that I just make you bored
I know I appear rather well jaded
As over the years my looks have faded

Our life together has been a tough ride
It's still the same old me inside
There's something that I always dread
That I'll no longer be welcome in your bed

I wish there was more that I could do
And that you'd love me like I love you
You no longer hug me or kiss me at all
You hide me away when your friends come to call

Another day passed, not a cuddle in sight
Tomorrow may change, I hope that it might
Guess I'll just have to wait till you're ready
After all I'm only a scruffy old teddy!

Julie Trainor

Anchor Books Information

We hope you have enjoyed reading this book - and that you will continue to enjoy it in the coming years.

If you like reading and writing poetry drop us a line, or give us a call, and we'll send you a free information pack.

Alternatively if you would like to order further copies of this book or any of our other titles, then please give us a call or log onto our website at
www.forwardpress.co.uk

Anchor Books Information
Remus House
Coltsfoot Drive
Peterborough
PE2 9JX

(01733) 898102